WOMEN in SPORTS

By Rebecca Phillips-Bartlett

BEARPORT
PUBLISHING

Minneapolis, Minnesota

Credits

All images are courtesy of Shutterstock.com, unless otherwise specified. With thanks to Getty Images, Thinkstock Photo, and iStockphoto. Cover – balabolka, Amma Shams. Throughout – balabolka, Amma Shams. 4–5 – PeopleImages.com - Yuri A. 6–7 – William J. Root, Chicago, Public domain, via Wikimedia Commons, Studio Tourne, Public domain, via Wikimedia Commons, Regina M art, Dooder, zizi_mentos. 8–9 – Bain News Service, publisher, Public domain, via Wikimedia Commons, Public domain, via Wikimedia Commons, Le Miroir des sports, Public domain, via Wikimedia Commons, mhatzapa, Elena Pimukova. 10–11 – File:Althea Gibson - El Gráfico 2033.jpg, Public domain, via Wikimedia Commons, Fred Palumbo (New York World-Telegram and the Sun staff photographer), Public domain, via Wikimedia Commons, zizi_mentos, balabolka, yukimco. 12–13 – Henk Lindeboom / Anefo, CC BY-SA 3.0 NL <https://creativecommons.org/licenses/by-sa/3.0/nl/deed.en>, via Wikimedia Commons, Joop van Bilsen / Anefo, CC0, via Wikimedia Commons, New York World-Telegram and the Sun Newspaper Photograph Collection, Public domain, via Wikimedia Commons. 14–15 – Boston Globe Marathona, CC BY-SA 3.0 <https://creativecommons.org/licenses/by-sa/3.0>, via Wikimedia Commons, Belikova Oksana, wasapohn, Witthawas Suknantee. 16–17 – blurAZ, flysnowfly, Artsaba Family, GoodStudio, frozenbunn, ilham arief, Mychal Watts. 18–19 – Featureflash Photo Agency, VectorsMarket, Kent Capture, CC BY 2.0 <https://creativecommons.org/licenses/by/2.0>, via Wikimedia Commons, Remo_Designer, Vector Point Studio, halimqd. 20–21 – Ray Terrill, CC BY-SA 2.0 <https://creativecommons.org/licenses/by-sa/2.0>, via Wikimedia Commons, Ailura, Derivative work by Ytoyoda, CC BY-SA 3.0 AT, CC BY-SA 3.0 AT <https://creativecommons.org/licenses/by-sa/3.0/at/deed.en>, via Wikimedia Commons, Ray Terrill, CC BY-SA 2.0 <https://creativecommons.org/licenses/by-sa/2.0>, via Wikimedia Commons, GoodStudio, puruan, Yevgen Kravchenko. 22–23 – Bollywood Hungama, CC BY 3.0 <https://creativecommons.org/licenses/by/3.0>, via Wikimedia Commons, Magnus D from London, United Kingdom, CC BY 2.0 <https://creativecommons.org/licenses/by/2.0>, via Wikimedia Commons, Ministry of Youth Affairs and Sports (GODL-India), GODL-India <https://data.gov.in/sites/default/files/Gazette_Notification_OGDL.pdf>, via Wikimedia Commons, Elena LAtkun, jenny on the moon. 24–25 – photofriday, Wojciech Migda (Wmigda), CC BY-SA 3.0 <https://creativecommons.org/licenses/by-sa/3.0>, via Wikimedia Commons, Chatchai Somwat, shopplaywood, Elena Pimukova. 26–27 – Laura_Dekker.JPG: Savyasachiderivative work: ukexpat, CC BY-SA 3.0 <https://creativecommons.org/licenses/by-sa/3.0>, via Wikimedia Commons, Lighthouse Roter Sand, CC BY-SA 3.0 <https://creativecommons.org/licenses/by-sa/3.0>, via Wikimedia Commons, Tim the Finn, zizi_mentos, Shmakova_creative. 28–29 – Underwood & Underwood (active 1880 – c. 1950)[1], Public domain, via Wikimedia Commons, Unknown photographer, Public domain, via Wikimedia Commons, Featureflash Photo Agency, Astarina, aushilfe444, OLIVIER MORIN/Getty Images.

Bearport Publishing Company Product Development Team

President: Jen Jenson; Director of Product Development: Spencer Brinker; Managing Editor: Allison Juda; Associate Editor: Naomi Reich; Associate Editor: Tiana Tran; Art Director: Colin O'Dea; Designer: Kim Jones; Designer: Kayla Eggert; Product Development Assistant: Owen Hamlin

Library of Congress Cataloging-in-Publication Data is available at www.loc.gov or upon request from the publisher.

ISBN: 979-8-88916-981-9 (hardcover)
ISBN: 979-8-89232-513-4 (paperback)
ISBN: 979-8-89232-165-5 (ebook)

For more information, write to Bearport Publishing, 5357 Penn Avenue South, Minneapolis, MN 55419.

Contents

She Who Dares

Some people love competitive sports, while other people enjoy working toward their own goals. However people play, sports can make them feel strong and healthy. From team games and solo sprints to heavy lifting and beautiful dances, playing sports is a great way to be active.

Every athlete has their own reason for playing sports. Some people use sports to show the world their abilities while others play just to have fun. There are even athletes who use sports to help other people.

There are many different kinds of sports and different ways to play them. What is your favorite way to be active?

SISTERS IN SPORTS

Throughout history, many women have faced challenges while trying to follow their athletic ambitions. Women have been banned from competing in all kinds of sports. Some people even thought women couldn't be as athletic as men.

Luckily, many daring women have broken through **barriers** to play sports and to set new records. They have used both their **physical** and mental strength to accomplish incredible things.

Breaking through barriers takes lots of bravery and courage.

How do you find strength to face the challenges in your life?

Annie Londonderry

SUPER CYCLIST

Born: 1870   **Died:** 1947

Annie Londonderry was born in Riga, Latvia. When she was five years old, she and her family moved to Boston, Massachusetts. By age 23, she was married and had three children. In 1894, Londonderry wanted to do something different.

Londonderry decided to ride a bicycle around the world. She had not cycled before. In fact, her first bike ride had been just two days before her big adventure! However, Londonderry was determined to show the world just how incredible women can be.

Londonderry's real name was Annie Cohen Kopchovsky. She rode under the name Londonderry to give recognition to the company that **sponsored** her journey.

Londonderry started her trip wearing skirts. However, the loose fabric of skirts made cycling much harder. Soon, she started wearing pants. Londonderry finished her biking journey wearing suits originally made for men.

A sand sculpture of Londonderry

Even though many people doubted her, Londonderry successfully traveled around the world in just 15 months. Her journey proved how strong and independent women could be. It also helped bring more attention to the women's rights movement.

Londonderry's journey inspired women to start cycling and to do things on their own.

Gertrude Ederle

CHANNEL-CROSSING CHAMPION

Born: 1905   **Died:** 2003

Gertrude Ederle was born in New York City. She learned to swim at her local pool. As she got older, she began training to become a professional swimmer.

Gertrude Ederle at the Olympics

Ederle won her first local competition when she was 16 years old. When she was 18, she swam in the 1924 Olympics and won three medals, including a gold medal.

Ederle wanted to swim further than the Olympic pools would allow. In 1925, she began training to cross the English Channel. Later that year, she tried to swim the channel but didn't make it across. Still, Ederle was determined to reach her goal. In August 1926, she succeeded. She was the first woman to swim across the English Channel!

Ederle swam the channel in 14 hours and 31 minutes. This was the fastest anyone had ever done it.

The part of the channel Ederle swam was 21 miles (34 km) wide. However, because of rough seas, she actually swam about 35 miles (56 km).

During her life, Ederle's hearing was damaged and she became **deaf.** After her successful swim across the channel, she taught swimming to children at the Lexington School for the Deaf.

Ederle was often called the Queen of the Waves.

Althea Gibson

WIMBLEDON WINNER

☆☆☆☆☆ **Born:** 1927   **Died:** 2003 ☆☆☆☆☆

Althea Gibson was born in Silver, South Carolina. When she was very young, her family moved to a neighborhood in New York City called Harlem. Gibson struggled at school. However, she was very good at sports.

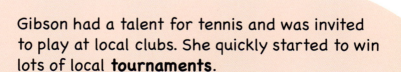

Gibson had a talent for tennis and was invited to play at local clubs. She quickly started to win lots of local **tournaments**.

At the time, **segregation** was everywhere in the United States. This meant that Gibson was not allowed to enter many tournaments because she was Black. But she didn't let this stop her from being her best. In 1942, she entered a tournament sponsored by the American Tennis Association—a group led by and for Black tennis players.

Between 1947 and 1956, Gibson won 10 **championships** in a row.

Gibson broke through many barriers and became the first Black player to enter huge international tournaments. Between 1956 and 1958, she won some of the biggest tennis competitions in the world, including the French Open, Wimbledon, and the U.S. Open.

Gibson also played golf. She was the first Black woman to compete on a professional golf tour.

Wilma Rudolph

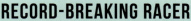

RECORD-BREAKING RACER

Born: 1940   **Died:** 1994

Wilma Rudolph was born in Clarksville, Tennessee. As a child, she had a disease that caused her left leg to become **paralyzed**. Doctors told her that she would never be able to walk again. However, Rudolph's parents and siblings worked hard to take care of her. Eventually, she was able to hop and then walk.

By age 11, Rudolph had become very athletic and enjoyed playing basketball. In high school, she joined the basketball team. However, she became better known for her speed. Rudolph was encouraged to try track and field.

When she was 16 years old, Rudolph competed in the 1956 Olympics and won a bronze medal. In 1960, she headed to the Olympics determined to get the gold. Rudolph won three gold medals and broke three world records!

Because of her 1960 Olympics success, people called Rudolph the fastest woman in the world.

Athletes often had homecoming parades to celebrate when they got home from big competitions. However, these events were usually segregated. Rudolph refused to attend a segregated homecoming parade. She used her sports success to stand up for **civil rights**.

Rudolph started an **organization** to help encourage young people to run. What group could you start to help others?

Kathrine Switzer

Born: 1947

Kathrine Switzer grew up in Fairfax County, Virginia. As a teenager, she ran every day. Running made her feel strong and **empowered**.

While at college, Switzer began training for longer runs. She entered the Boston Marathon in 1967. At the time, the marathon was considered a male-only event. However, there were no rules that said women could not enter. So, Switzer pinned on her race number 261 and started running.

261

During the race, the people in charge realized Switzer was a woman and tried to remove her from the course. But other runners nearby did not let this happen. Switzer became the first woman to run Boston Marathon with an official race number.

Switzer at the 2017 Boston Marathon

In 2017, 50 years after her groundbreaking marathon run, Switzer ran the Boston Marathon again. She was 70 years old at the time.

Boston Marathon officially started accepting women in 1972.

Switzer changed the history of women in running. In 1977, she started a series of women's races called the Avon International Running Circuit. This helped pave the way for the women's marathon to become an Olympic event. Switzer encourages other women to run in the hope that they might find the same empowerment she did.

261

Candace Cable

Born: 1954

Candace Cable was born in Glendale, California. Growing up, she loved hiking and skiing. But when she was 21 years old, she was badly injured in a car accident and could no longer walk. Candace felt lonely and decided to get help figuring out ways she could still be active.

During college, Cable was involved with the Disabled Student Services group. This gave her the opportunity to try a variety of sports. After trying a few different things, she took part in a wheelchair race. Cable had finally found her sport!

Wheelchair racing was still very new at the time, so Cable helped design the equipment and create the rules.

Cable trained very hard. In 1980, she raced at the summer **Paralympics** and won two gold medals. In 1992, she won two other medals at the winter Paralympics. She was the first woman to win at both the Summer and Winter Games.

Cable has won 84 marathons!

In addition to her dominance in sports, Cable has dedicated herself to helping others. After her injury, she felt as though she didn't have any role models. So, she became a role model for others. She also **advocates** for the rights of people with disabilities.

Cable wants to be a role model for others. What does being a role model mean to you?

Nicola Adams

Born: 1982

Nicola Adams was born in Leeds, England. Growing up, she watched videos of great boxers, but they were all men. When she was 12 years old, Adams began taking boxing lessons at a local gym. About a year later, she had her first competitive boxing match and won! In that moment, Adams decided she was going to win an Olympic gold medal in boxing. However, women's boxing wasn't even a sport at the Olympics yet.

Adams worked toward her dream. In 2001, she became the first female boxer to fight for England. She later became the country's **amateur** champion.

Finally, in 2009, it was announced that women's boxing would be an event at the next Olympics. Adams got a place on Great Britain's first women's Olympic boxing team. In 2012, she became the first woman to win an Olympic gold medal in boxing.

Along with being the first woman to win in an Olympic ring, Adams was also the first openly **LGBTQ** person to win a medal in boxing. She continues to use her fame and success to speak out about her experiences and to stand up for LGBTQ people's rights.

Adams has won every major boxing title available, including European and World Champion!

Nadia Nadim

SOCCER STAR AND SURGEON

Born: 1988

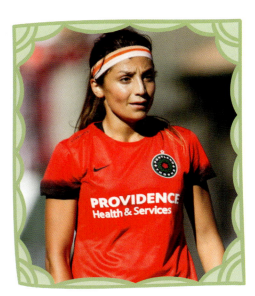

Nadia Nadim was born in Herat, Afghanistan. When she was just 11 years old, her father was killed by a **terrorist** group called the Taliban. Nadim, her four sisters, and their mother left the country and escaped to Denmark. While living in a **refugee camp**, she saw people playing soccer and decided that she wanted to join in the fun.

Playing soccer made Nadim feel happy and free. Eventually, she became a professional soccer player. She has played on teams for Manchester City, Paris Saint-Germain, and Denmark.

Nadim playing for Denmark

Nadim uses her fame to help people who come from backgrounds similar to hers. She works with charities to encourage children to play sports and to help women and girls get a good education.

Even though soccer is her career, Nadim loves the sport so much that she doesn't think of it as a job. In between matches, she trained to be a surgeon. Whether as a star on the field or in the operating room, Nadim wants to encourage and help other people.

Nadim can speak nine languages!

Geeta Phogat and Babita Kumari Phogat

Born: 1988

Geeta Phogat

Born: 1989

Babita Kumari Phogat

Geeta and Babita Kumari Phogat are sisters who were born in Haryana, India. Their dad was a wrestling coach and trained them in the sport. Even though there were many famous Indian wrestlers, they were all men. The sisters didn't have a role model to look up to.

The sisters trained for many years. Their first big break into wrestling came at the 2010 Commonwealth Games. The sisters competed in different weight categories. Geeta Phogat made history when she won a gold medal. This was India's first Commonwealth gold in women's wrestling.

Geeta Phogat's winning fight in 2010

The younger Phogat sister had her own big victory at the games. She won a silver medal in her weight category. Just four years later, she won a gold medal in the same category her older sister had previously dominated.

In 2012, Geeta Phogat became the first Indian woman wrestler to qualify for the Olympics. The Phogat sisters have fought against **stereotypes** and brought more attention to women's wrestling.

The 2012 London Olympic Stadium

Yani Tseng

GOLFING GLORY

Born: 1989

Yani Tseng was born in Taiwan. She always loved sports and began playing golf when she was just six years old. This early start helped pave the way for her record-breaking career.

When she was young, Tseng trained very hard to become a golf star. In 2003, she won the Callaway Junior World Golf Championships for girls ages 13 to 14.

One of Tseng's early wins in 2010

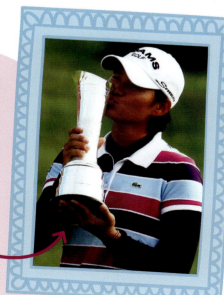

By 2007, Tseng was a professional golfer. She became the youngest person ever to win five major championships.

For more than two years, Tseng was ranked the number one player in the Women's World Golf Rankings. In 2012, *Time* magazine included her in a list of the top 100 most influential people in the world.

Laura Dekker

YOUNGEST SOLO SAILOR

Born: 1995

Laura Dekker was born in Whangarei, New Zealand during her parents' seven-year sailing trip. Her early start on the water meant that she has always felt at home on the ocean.

After the family returned to the Netherlands, Dekker's dad started building his own boat. Dekker helped and was inspired to build her own sailing raft when she was just six years old. A couple of years later, she decided that she wanted to sail the world and began training.

Set on making her dream a reality, 10-year-old Dekker fixed up a friend's boat and used it to sail around Holland and the Wadden Islands. She had no other people with her, though she was not completely alone. She took her dog Spot on the trip.

The boat Dekker sailed on was called *Guppy*.

At 14 years old, Dekker had her biggest adventure yet—she set off to sail the seas. She returned nearly two years later and had become the youngest person to sail solo around the world!

Dekker's trip taught her self-confidence and how to be brave.

More Daring Women

AMELIA EARHART and Her Fearless Flights

Born: 1897   **Died:** Around 1937

In 1932, Amelia Earhart became the first woman to fly across the Atlantic Ocean. She faced lots of issues with the weather and her plane during the journey, but she worked hard and completed the trip.

MARIA TALLCHIEF and Her Bold Ballet

Born: 1925   **Died:** 2013

Maria Tallchief was born in Fairfax, Oklahoma, and was a member of the Osage tribe. She began learning ballet when she was just three years old. As an adult, she became the star of many ballet companies and was recognized for her amazing **technique** and strength.

Tallchief is remembered for breaking down barriers for Native American women.

ROBINA MUQIMYAR and Her Rebellious Runs

Born: 1986

When Robina Muqimyar was young, she lived under Taliban control. This meant she was banned from taking part in sports. However, she did not let this hold her back. In 2004, Muqimyar ran at the Olympics. She became one of the first women to represent Afghanistan at the Olympic Games.

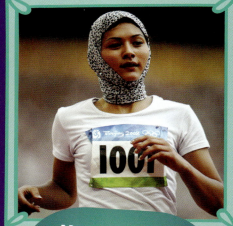

Muqimyar wears a hijab, or traditional Muslim headscarf, when she runs.

ELLIE SIMMONDS and Her Strong Swimming

Born: 1994

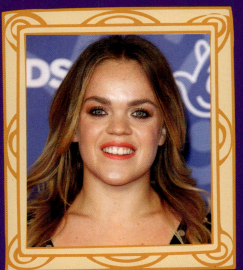

Ellie Simmonds was born with a condition that affects her growth. She first started swimming when she was about five years old. By age 13, she had won 2 Paralympic gold medals. Simmonds was one of the youngest British Paralympians to win a medal.

Changing the World

Many women have trained and worked very hard to become sports stars. Whether they were breaking records, doing things that no one had done before, or working toward their own amazing goals, the world would not be the same without women in sports!

Achieving amazing things can be very challenging. However, these women had the determination and strength to break through the barriers that blocked their paths. They dared to be different so they could change the world.

DO YOU DARE TO CHANGE THE WORLD?

Sports stars often try many sports before they find the one they love. What new sport would you like to try?

Glossary

advocates supports or speaks in favor of something

amateur an athlete who is not a professional and doesn't receive money for performing

barriers obstacles that block or limit access to something

championships contests or final games of a series that decide which player or team will be the winner

civil rights rights that each person has to be treated equally

deaf not able to hear

empowered had the confidence to do things or make decisions

LGBTQ an abbreviation for lesbian, gay, bisexual, transgender, and queer, which represents people from a variety of gender identities and sexual orientations

organization a group of people with a common interest or purpose

Paralympics international contests, associated with the Olympics, for athletes with disabilities

paralyzed made unable to move parts of the body

physical to do with the body

refugee camp temporary camps where people who have been forced to leave their homes can take shelter

segregation a forced separation of people, often by race

sponsored paid money to support an activity

stereotypes sets of harmful ideas about how people from a specific group will behave

technique a way of doing something

terrorist having to do with individuals or groups that use violence and fear to get what they want

tournaments sporting events with a series of games or rounds

INDEX

READ MORE

Levit, Joseph. *Gymnastics's G.O.A.T: Nadia Comaneci, Simone Biles, and More (Sports' Greatest of All Time)*. Minneapolis: Lerner Publications, 2022.

Rosen, Karen. *Trailblazing Women in Track and Field (Trailblazing Female Athletes)*. Chicago: Norwood House Press, 2023.

Sher, Abby. *Champions: 25 Tales of Unstoppable Athletes (Rebel Girls)*. Mankato, MN: Black Rabbit Books, 2024.

LEARN MORE ONLINE

1. Go to **www.factsurfer.com** or scan the QR code below.
2. Enter "**Women in Sports**" into the search box.
3. Click on the cover of this book to see a list of websites.